eBay

Complete Step-By-Step Beginners Guide to Start a Profitable and Sustainable eBay Business

By
Shea Hendricks

© 2016

Table of Contents

Preface

Chapter 1: An Introduction to Selling on eBay

Chapter 2: Starting your eBay Business

Chapter 3: Understanding How to sell on eBay

Chapter 4: A Guide to the Products to sell on eBay

Chapter 5: Create a Proper Listing

Chapter 6: Promote your eBay Business for Success

Conclusion

Preface

When we talk about online shopping, eBay is easily one of the leading names in the market. As such, selling products on this site can actually be a great business idea. On the other hand, you need to know how to run it properly. After all, you will want it to become a massive success. This is where this book comes in.

In this book, you will be learning the ropes about running a business on eBay. This platform certainly provides a lot of support to sellers and buyers alike. Unfortunately, that is not enough to run a business. After all, there are many things to take care of. You will come to know about them in this book.

You will get to understand eBay and tips for getting your feet wet in the platform. Once you are ready, you are going to be guided through the process of setting up the legal and administrative sides of the business.

Then, you will be learning about the different kinds of products that you can sell in the platforms. Tips will also be provided for the sources you can utilize in order to get the products for selling.

Finally, you will be reading about the best way to list your products and promoting them for continued success. After all, promotion and advertisement is vital to the visibility and success of any business and an eBay business is no different.

I hope this book proves to be useful for you in helping you to start your very own eBay business. Let's now start on this incredible journey.

Chapter 1: An Introduction to Selling on eBay

When you want to start a business, you need to think about a channel through which you can sell your products. One of the best channels you can utilize is eBay. After all, it is available in 190 countries around the world and serves over 165 million buyers. As such, it can be an excellent platform for sellers.

Even better is the fact that you can use eBay exclusively for running your business. After all, it already has customers lined up for you to sell your products to. It even provides the support and solutions you require to succeed at your business.

Understanding eBay
While running an eBay business is a great idea, it is not easy to do so unless you know what it is you are getting into. The first thing you need to understand about this platform is what it is not.

You should never expect eBay to provide you with a business that you just need to start running. In other words, you cannot click on a button and magically get a business to run. At the same time, an eBay business is not like your regular businesses that use stores to sell products on. At the same time, you cannot join eBay and learn how to run a business before starting one.

The fact is eBay is a platform where people come together to buy and sell products. People can visit the site and browse through the products offered by various sellers and buy what they need or want. Others visit eBay to sell their products. It is even possible to do both of these activities at the same time.

You should think of eBay as a store in a mall. The mall owners simply provide you a space with. It becomes your responsibility to fill up that space with products and items for selling to the customer. It is also your responsibility to find the products and determine their prices. Finally, you are liable for delivering the purchased items to your buyers.

Therefore, an eBay business will take some time, lots of effort and considerable research if you want to it to be a resounding success.

However, there are a few things about an eBay business that makes it similar to any regular business. For example, reputation can go a long way in helping you to become a successful seller. Additionally, the quality of your service can determine whether buyers will be likely to return for another purchase.

Starting with eBay
Building a business with eBay is just as difficult as developing any other business. As long as you understand this, you will find it easier to approach the process of selling on eBay. Of course, you need to start thinking like an entrepreneur and have some sense of business. Good communication skills can also be quite helpful in this matter. Try and develop these skills as they can be essential for your survival on eBay. After all, it is just as competitive as any other marketplace.

Now that you understand what you need to possess, you can take the first step towards building your business on eBay.

First, you need to join eBay if you have not already done so. The good thing is that eBay offers only one kind of account and that account can be made for free. You can use the same account for purchasing and selling items on eBay. Take your time to understand the different features and options available for your account.

Buy and Sell a Few Items
Once you have understood your account, you should go ahead and make a few purchases and then sell a few items. This will help you get acquainted with both sides of the equation.

Make a few purchases first. Search for items that you require or want. There is no need to spend a lot of money in these purchases. After all, you are simply researching the activity. Check the product listings under different formats. Items are sold in eBay in different formats.

The basic format is the fixed price listings. You simply pay the amount of money listed for the item and buy it by clicking on the Buy It Now button. This is the easiest format and one that you are certainly going to be using when you sell items. In some fixed price listings, an option called Best Offer is also available. Using this option, you can make an offer to the seller for the product. If the seller likes the offer you have placed, you can get the item for the price that you offered.

Auctions are quite popular among eBay buyers. These listings last for a specific period of time, from a few hours to a few days. Buyers bid on the item. The auction closes after the time limit expires. The highest bid at the closure of the auction is declared to be the winning bid and the buyer who made the bid receives the item. It is possible to bid on the listing time more than once and increase it in order to win the item.

Sometimes, sellers can also include a Buy It Now price with auctions enabling buyers to pay a set amount of money get the item. As such, they do not have to go through the hassles of auctioning. Some sellers also include a Best Offer option in the same listing.

As you buy items through these kinds of listings, you get a good idea as to how people shop on eBay. Understanding the purchase process can help you considerably when you start selling. Being a buyer yourself, you will know what buyers look for in a listing. As a result, you can ensure that your own listings have been created properly.

Before making your purchase, make sure that you check all the details completely. You need to ensure that you are satisfied with the item descriptions and condition. The delivery time must also be checked. You must also have a look at the seller rating to understand whether the seller is worth doing business with. These details should guide you as you try to understand the suitability and the quality of the item.

Once you have bought a few items, you should start selling a few items. At first, you should list only item. That item can be anything that is allowed under eBay guidelines. You can easily find a few items worth selling around your house. You can use lists of items that can be sold in eBay by first time sellers. You can sell any items that you do not need.

For selling, you need to click on the sell button. You will then need to fill up an online form. Keep in mind that having images of the product can make it easier to sell it. The images should be at least of a good quality so as to attract customers. Once done, you can post the listing for people to buy from. Make sure that you create a compelling listing as they can increase the chances of your product being sold. Do not forget to mention the item condition and add an item description.

Once a buyer purchases the item, package the item and ship it to the address. Make sure that you have received the payment first. Once the buyer receives the item, they should leave feedback for you. If they do not, you can certainly ask and request them to do so. Seller feedback can be vital to your success.

Is eBay Suitable for You?

After experiencing a few purchases and sales, you should take a look at the different rules that exist for sellers. These rules are discussed later in this book. Then, think back to the experiences that you had while purchasing and, more importantly, while selling the items. Did you enjoy the process? Can you see yourself running a business for the long-term in eBay?

Remember that it will take time before your eBay business establishes itself properly. It may even take months for that to happen. In this aspect, it is just like any other business that you can run. You must never have an unreal expectation that you can get rich quickly simply because you are using eBay. There can be difficult times ahead for you and you may have to suffer hardships before you can enjoy the taste of success.

Undertake a careful consideration of all these factors. Finally, determine whether this will be the right choice for you. If you are satisfied with all the aspects of running an eBay business, you can start taking the necessary steps to make it a reality.

Chapter 2: Starting your eBay Business

You have already sold a few items in eBay. However, that does not mean that you can just dive into the site and create a business. Simply selling more items to earn money is not the philosophy that you should be following. In order to ensure that your business survives in the long term while bringing in a steady source of profit, you have to start thinking like a businessman.

Ensure the Legality of Your Business
You can easily sell items on eBay. There will not be any issues if you are selling items only once in a while. On the other hand, you will have to sell more items on a regular basis if you want run a business. Your aim is to generate profit after all. As such, the law will treat your transactions on eBay as business transactions and view your activity as that of a business.

Of course, businesses are subject to regulations and rules by law. An eBay business will have to follow these laws if it wants to keep thriving. Failure to comply with the regulations can have severe repercussions. Depending on the laws in force in your location, you may have to face fines or incur heavier penalties. Some of the laws you may need to take a look at are given below.

Zoning Laws

Many governments tend to designate certain locations and areas as a specific zone. Some zones give you the ability to conduct business while doing so in other zones may be considered illegal. As a result, you may not have the right to conduct an eBay business from your home if your home falls into a non-commercial zone.

Do not labor under the misconception that no one will find out that you are running a business from your home. Your neighbors might notice the shipments and the trucks, if you are using them. They may even complain about it. As a result, you should check out the zoning laws in your area and see what you need to do get permission. In few cases, you may do not have any choice but shift the location of your business.

Licensing Laws

The majority of the countries and areas where eBay is accessible tend to have licensing laws. As such, you need to get a license for your eBay business, register it in a directory or something similar. If your business has not been licensed or registered, it can become subject to fines or even closure.

Tax Laws

Tax is another reason why you need to go the legal route when starting an eBay business. This is also the reason why your operation needs to be licensed and registered. There can be a variety of taxes applicable for your business, depending on its scale and profit margins. If you have not been registered or licensed, the government can place fines on your business apart from collecting the back taxes. In short, you may end up paying a lot of money that could have been avoided easily.

Employment Laws

If you have people to help you with your eBay business, local laws may consider them to be your employees even if you do not. Therefore, your business will need to follow the employment regulations as per the local laws.

Other Laws

Some of the other laws that you may have to follow include those on consumer protection, insurance and liability. These laws are meant to protect the buyers and the public in general from any negligent action undertaken by a business. These laws can differ from place to place. These laws may prevent you from selling or sourcing specific types of products. Their handling or disclaimers may also be governed by such laws. You must ensure that you are compliant with those laws as applicable to prevent severe penalties and fines from being applied to your business.

If you want to ensure the continued success of your eBay business, you need to keep an eye on these laws. Contact the local office of your government as soon as possible to complete the formalities. There can be lots of paperwork to take care of. However, doing them now can save you a lot of trouble down the line.

Fundamental Steps in Starting the Business
Once you have ensured the legality of your eBay business, there will still be a few things

that you need to take care of. These are administrative tasks that will ensure that your business keeps running every day in the smoothest manner possible.

Insurance

Once your business has grown past a certain limit, you will find that your inventory has been substantial. As such, a lot of money will have gotten tied into your business. When this happens, you need to seek insurance for your business. By doing insurance, you will make sure that you do not end up incurring a significant financial loss in case of disasters. After all, accidents, whether manmade or natural, can occur any time without warning. For extremely large inventories, insurance becomes unavoidable. Remember that homeowner's insurance may not cover your eBay business even if you run it from your home.

Office

All businesses require a headquarters or an office at the very least to operate from. You may create an office at your own home or rent a space. An office can make it much easier to run your eBay business.

When creating an office, ensure that distractions are minimal. After all, you are going to run a business. You should also look into the legal and taxation aspects of running an office at home. Furnish the office with the essentials and get a separate computer system with its own broadband internet connection.

You will also require a shipping area and a storage area for your inventory. Depending on the items you are planning on selling and the volume of sales, you may have to consider purchasing or renting a separate storage area. In fact, doing so will be better as it can lessen the noise and confusion at your home when you ship the items. Organize the area properly so that the workflow can be as smooth as possible.

To sell your products on eBay, you need to take photographs. As such, you may want to consider creating a separate area for the taking photographs of your products. The photo area should be stocked with all the essentials and completely modified to suit the purpose.

Records

It is absolutely important for the success of your business that you maintain immaculate records. There are various tools that you can use from a simple paper ledger to complex business management systems. In the beginning, paper ledgers or spreadsheet applications like Microsoft Excel will be enough.

If you do know bookkeeping and record maintenance, you need to learn how to do so as soon as possible. The accuracy of these records is vital especially when you are filing for taxes or getting insurance. Make sure that you track all aspects such as the purchases, sales, prices, delivery costs, shipping times, sale times, refunds, so on and so forth.

Chapter 3: Understanding How to sell on eBay

When you want to sell on eBay, you need an account first and then start listing products. This model may work well when you are simply selling one or two items every once in a while. On the other hand, it is completely unsuitable for running an eBay business with. Here are a few things you need to take care of so as to ensure the best possible results for your sale.

Maintain an About Me Page
In eBay, all members have the option to create an About Me page for free. This is an HTML-based space which can be used for providing information about your business. Many sellers do not make use of this feature but established members understand its importance and ensure that the page is maintained properly.

Remember that the About Me page will be linked to your eBay member ID. Therefore, it will appear as an icon beside your ID wherever your ID is mentioned on eBay. Here are some of the things that you should consider implementing in the page.

Auctions and Listings: The primary use of this page has been to provide links to the auctions and the listings that you are currently running on eBay. This allows buyers to find those items easily from your About Me.

Testimonials: You can add links to the best feedback that you have received from your previous customers. After all, buyers do go through the feedback before purchasing.

Transactional Information: There will be quite a few details that are common to all your listings. Your return policies, shipping information and contact details are some of them. You can mention such information on the About Me page as well to help the buyers and bidders.

Logo: If you have a company logo, you can add it to this page. It can significantly help in building brand recognition.

Developing a Good Feedback Profile

Unlike other ecommerce sites, feedback is strongly encouraged in eBay. In fact, the majority of buyers will first check the feedback and the rating of the seller before they actually purchase anything from that seller. As a result, your feedback profile has to be a strong one if you want to run a successful eBay business.

In fact, you will certainly be trying to get lots of feedback from your buyers. Of course, it will take time to build your feedback and ratings. As such, you should try to get some feedback at the very least when you have started selling products. Here are a few tips to help you get started with a feedback profile.

Buy Items

Even if your goal is to start selling items, you can purchase a few products first. Sellers can also leave feedback for the buyers. For this reason, you can easily build up your feedback profile before you can start selling. You can purchase common items that you are going to need in your home or office such as stationary goods like pens and basic kitchen utensils such as spoons and mugs. These can be bought cheaply allowing you to gather a sizeable amount of feedback in a short period of time.

Prepare for a Sale

You should only list your items when you are ready to sell them. As such, you should have them packaged for shipping. Find out the working hours and holidays of the shipping companies so that you can ship the items at the right time once they are sold. This will ensure that your buyers get the items within the specified time frame which increases the chances of them leaving positive feedback ratings.

Start Small

When you are starting off as a seller, you should stick to small products. Avoid selling any items of a high value when you are just starting. After all, you need to have a high feedback in order to attract bids of a high value. By selling items of a smaller value, you can increase the number of sales you make as they require less investment. With more sales you will be getting more feedback.

Ask for Feedback
Since you are trying to build a good feedback profile as quickly as possible, you should be asking the buyers to provide you with some. Typically, experienced buyers will provide feedback on their own accord within a few days after they receive the item. If you find that the buyer has not left a feedback even after the transaction was concluded successfully, you can send them a request to do so. This is allowed by eBay so you don't have to worry about spamming as long as you don't send them more than one request. You should also leave some feedback for the buyer in order to encourage them to do the same.

Be Trustworthy
Trustworthy sellers can easily maintain a feedback rating higher than 90%. This is

because they are ethical and contentious in their approach to selling items on eBay. Try to keep the buyer happy by clarifying all details about the item in the listing and answering their queries as soon as possible. Ensure that the delivery times have been mentioned correctly.

These things should help you get started with a good seller profile on eBay. Do not forget that these things need to be maintained regularly so as to ensure the best possible results for your eBay business.

Chapter 4: A Guide to the Products to sell on eBay

Unless you already have a manufacturing business that makes products for sale, you will be wondering what kind of items you can sell through eBay. The fact is that eBay allows nearly all kind of products to be sold on its platform. As a result, this can be a difficult choice to make.

However, it is not just the kind of products you want to sell that matter. You will also need to think about where you are going to get the products from. After all, you are not going to be making the products on your own. Here are a few tips to help you with these considerations.

Types of Products to Sell

As mentioned earlier, you can sell nearly all kinds of items on eBay as long as they are not illegal, dangerous or banned under eBay guidelines. Products being sold on eBay can be classified broadly into four categories.

Items in High Demand
These are hot items that are witnessing a lot of sales in the current period of time. Therefore, you are certain to get a lot of sales if you offer them. On the other hand, you need to constantly monitor product releases and their reception in order to know whose popularity is on the rise.

You will certainly require a good source in order to deliver these products to your own customers via eBay. A good idea for these products is to find those that are in short supply elsewhere. Products that are not yet released in other areas will also work. Of course, you need to ensure that the retail stores or wholesale clubs near you have an ample stock so that you can purchase the product in bulk to offset costs.

Items Similar To Those in High Demand
It is a fact of business that for every product with a high demand, there will be a number of

similar products on offer. These products are typically sold at a lower price or they have a feature point better than the original. There is actually a sizeable market for such products. Therefore, you should have no problems in finding customers.

You should certainly keep a track of the hottest products on the market. At the same time, search for clones or knock-offs for these products along with value-oriented editions. You can find such products at specialty retailers, wholesale lots, drop shippers and importers. Sometimes, you may even find them at Amazon and other online retailers.

Related Parts and Accessories
There are many products which require the use of parts and accessories. These extras can prove to be an excellent source of profit. As such, it is a popular idea used by many eBay sellers. You should first look in the possible accessories and parts that a hot product may have. Broaden your search to include multiple categories. Make a list and search your sources for those items. Any product that can be accessorized is certain to have a thriving market for such parts. You can search for these products in wholesale lots and drop shippers.

Popular Culture and Seasonal Items

These items are more of a fad than something that you can sell any time. They become popular for a short period of time as the subject they are based on captures public interest. Few of them may go on to be saleable years after the original fad has passed but most tend to be popular for a short while only.

Movie props are a good example of pop culture items. It is quite easy to get these items for sale. However, you should always remember that the window of popularity tends to be short. In order to discover which products will be popular at the moment, you have to keep a track of pop culture such as events and movies. For seasonal items, it becomes easier as you know which items will be popular at which time of the year. For example, costumes will always be in high demand during the Halloween season.

Research is vital for all products as is timing. You need to remain ahead of the market if you want to ensure a good profit. If you mistimed your sales, you can end up lose a lot of money by selling items at a low amount or not at all.

With experience, this will become easier for you.

Sourcing Products for Sale
If you want to turn a good profit in your eBay business, you need to get the products you sell at low prices. This is possible when you have the right sources to get them from. The good thing is that there is a wide variety of sources to choose from.

From Swap Meets and Flea Markets
You can meet a lot of local manufacturers and sellers at these places. They often offer a wide variety of products at a low price. You can easily pick some good collectibles and other interesting items here. Of course, you may have to spend some in finding products that will actually sell. In some cases, you may have to restore or clean the item before selling. Nonetheless, you can actually make a good profit this way.

From Drop Shippers
This is one of the most popular sources for many eBay businesses. You can easily find a number of them online. However, it can be difficult to make this model for your business. On the other hand, if you are willing to put in

enough effort, you may end up with a profitable source for selling on eBay.

From Thrift Stores

It is quite easy to find such stores scattered all over the city. You can easily find exciting products to sell on eBay at these stores at very low prices. You should visit a number of these stores on a regular basis. Some eBay sellers are known to make a round of these stores daily or multiple times in a week so that they do not miss out on anything.

From Online Retailers

There is no reason why you cannot find good products at online retailers for selling on eBay. However, you should not only browse through the popular ones. Search for online retailers that less well-known. More importantly, keep a track of their sales, deals, clearance items and any other discounts they are offering. These are great opportunities as you can later sell the items at full price on eBay.

From eBay

That is right. You can actually purchase items on eBay and then sell them again on the same platform. However, for this trick to work, you need to buy wholesale items. Then, you can break up the collection and sell each item individually on eBay. Alternatively, you can sell them on the other shopping properties owned by eBay such as Half.com and others.

These ideas should help you in sourcing the right products at the right process so that your business can actually be profitable. As you become a more experienced seller, you can discover more kinds of products to sell and sources to use.

Chapter 5: Create a Proper Listing

Like all businesses, you need to know how to sell a product properly if you want to turn a profit for your eBay business. For other business, you can take the help of promotional materials and ads to sell your items. This is not possible in eBay. On the other hand, you can increase the sale of your products by creating a good listing for it. In fact, the listing can even affect the performance of your auctions.

Check the Prices

You need to offer your products at the right price. If you keep it too low, you will certainly sell a lot of products but you will not be earning enough money. At the same time, it should not be so high that you are priced out of the market. Before you put the price on your product, you need to keep a few things in mind

Market Research: This is essential to ensuring that your products are being sold at the right prices. Use the advanced search function of eBay to find out the prices at which items similar to you have been sold. Use the 'completed listings only' option to help you in your search.

Auctions: When you are offering products through auction, you should keep the opening price of the item as cheap as possible. It has been repeatedly noticed that auctions with a low opening price attracts a lot of bids. As a result, they are sold at higher prices. On the other hand, auctions starting off with a high opening price will attract fewer products. Therefore, the final price at which they are sold is low. You should also remember that most bids take place in the final two hours or so for auctions.

Ensure the Right Duration

When selling products, you should keep the time limits of the listing as long as possible. More importantly, you should be posting such listings at the right time. The time is all the more important for auctions. By listing a few items with different durations, you can gain a good idea as to the right time frame for your product listings.

Describe the Items Correctly

The item descriptions provided in the listings should be complete and informative. Buyers should get enough information about the product to evaluate its purchase. If they are not getting enough details, most buyers will not be purchasing your items. To improve results, ensure that you have included a clear image of the actual product being sold. Keep the resolution large and take pictures from different angles to give the buyers a proper idea.

Experience is invaluable when selling on eBay. With time, you will understand what constitutes a good listing and improve your sales as a result.

Chapter 6: Promote your eBay Business for Success

A business needs to be promoted correctly and widely if it wants to be successful. That is why you find so many advertisements for products all around you. This is also the case for an eBay business. On the other hand, promoting a product on eBay is quite different from promoting other businesses. Here are some ideas you can implement.

Start Cross-Promotion
One of the best ways to increase the visibility of your products is through cross-promotion. In this technique, you will be including text and links to the other auctions and products that you have currently listed on eBay in the item description for one listing. Add as many products to the description as possible. Do not forget to ask the buyers to take a look at those products by mentioning it textually. Keep the text large and attractive. Do this for all of your products.

Use Multiple Categories
When you are listing your product, you should be putting it in multiple categories. After all, it is certainly possible that your product can be categorized in different ways. For example, a ring can be categorized under men's jewelry or fashion jewelry. At the same time, you can try selling multiple items in different categories. Of course, you must always ensure that the categories are all relevant. You can also cross-promote them

The idea is to bring in a wide range of potential buyers so that they become aware of your business. You can also list a few items that are in high demand so that they can be seen by more buyers. This will help buyers become familiar with your business.

Develop a Base of Repeat Customers
Even after you have listed the product, there are a few things that you can do to promote your business. At every stage of the purchase process, you have the opportunity to promote your business to the buyer. You can send your buyers an email with an invoice and links to your eBay store and other products. Do not forget to have your own letterhead for the invoices so that you can advertise your store.

If you really want to improve your promotion tactics, you can consider adding small gifts to each package. It can be something inexpensive such as a packet of mints. You will be surprised at the repeat business that you are generating by this simple tactic.

There many other techniques you can use for promoting such as social media. Keep an eye out for these techniques and start using them wherever possible.

Conclusion

Now that we have reached the end of this book, it helps to take a look back and see what we have learned. After all, it is a business we are talking about.

You now know that eBay does not provide readymade businesses for you to use. Instead, you need to work at developing it. The legal aspects such as licensing and taxation have been discussed so that your eBay business does not suffer from the law.

You will now be familiar with the different aspects of selling products on eBay such as the development of a strong feedback profile. You also know what kind of products can be sold through your eBay business and the sources you can get them from. Techniques for listing products and promoting your business should now be known to you now.

I hope this book has been useful to you in setting up your eBay business. I wish you all the best for your future in this business.

www.ingramcontent.com/pod-product-compliance
Lightning Source LLC
Chambersburg PA
CBHW070421190526
45169CB00003B/1357